MOVIE INSTRUMENTAL SOLOS

Project Manager: Zobeida Pérez
Book Cover and Design: JP Creative Group
Audio created and recorded by Artemis Music Limited
Arranged by Bill Galliford, Ethan Neuburg and Tod Edmondson

MOVIE INSTRUMENTAL SOLOS

Contents

HEDWIG'S THEME

Music by **JOHN WILLIAMS**

ACROSS THE STARS
(LOVE THEME FROM *STAR WARS*®: EPISODE II)

Music by
JOHN WILLIAMS

Appassionato

poco rit.

a tempo

rit. e dim.

DUEL OF THE FATES

Music by **JOHN WILLIAMS**

Duel of the Fates - 2 - 1
IFM0310CD

FAWKES THE PHOENIX

Music by **JOHN WILLIAMS**

Fawkes the Phoenix - 2 - 1
IFM0310CD

*An easier 8th-note alternative figure has been provided.

GOLLUM'S SONG

Words by FRAN WALSH
Music by HOWARD SHORE

Slowly, flowing (♩ = 52)

Gollum's Song - 2 - 1
IFM0310CD

OCTOBER SKY

Composed by
MARK ISHAM

October Sky - 2 - 1
IFM0310CD

SOUL BOSSA NOVA

Music by
QUINCY JONES

* An easier 8th-note alternative figure has been provided.

Soul Bossa Nova - 2 - 1
IFM0310CD

THERE YOU'LL BE

Words and Music by
DIANE WARREN

There You'll Be - 2 - 1
IFM0310CD

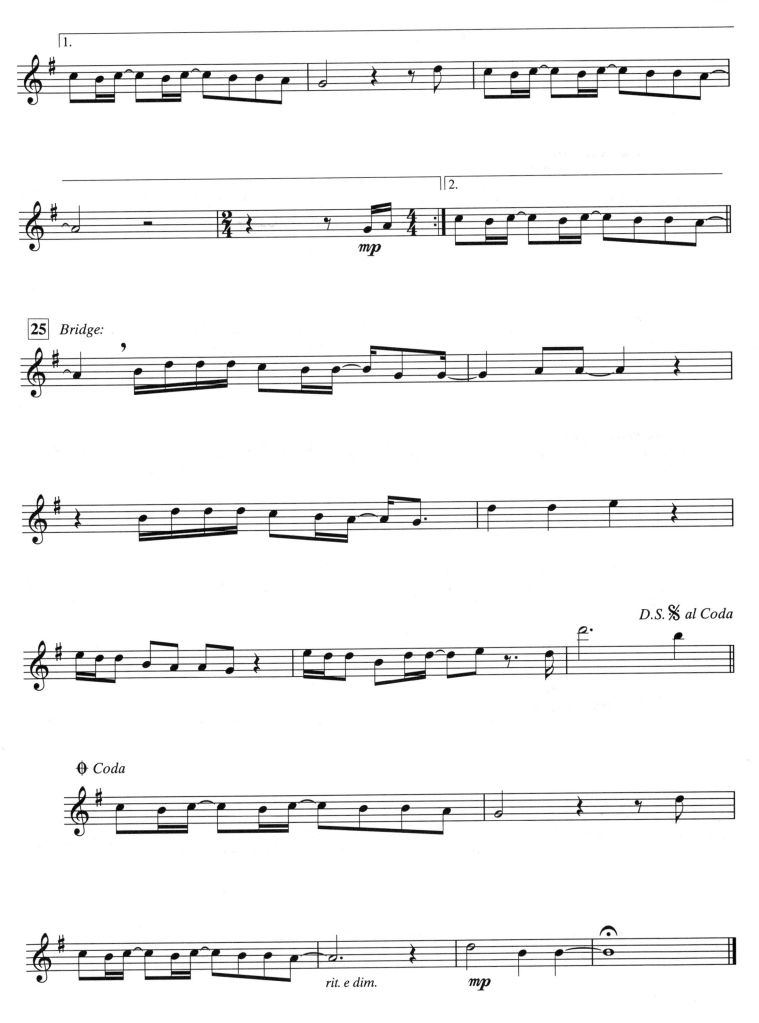

JAMES BOND THEME
Die Another Day

Music by MONTY NORMAN

IFM0310CD

IN DREAMS

Words and Music by
FRAN WALSH and
HOWARD SHORE

PARTS OF AN ALTO SAXOPHONE
AND FINGERING CHART

• When there are two fingerings given for a note, use the first one unless the alternate fingering is suggested.

• When two enharmonic notes are given together (F♯ and B♭ for example,) they sound the same pitch and are played the same way.

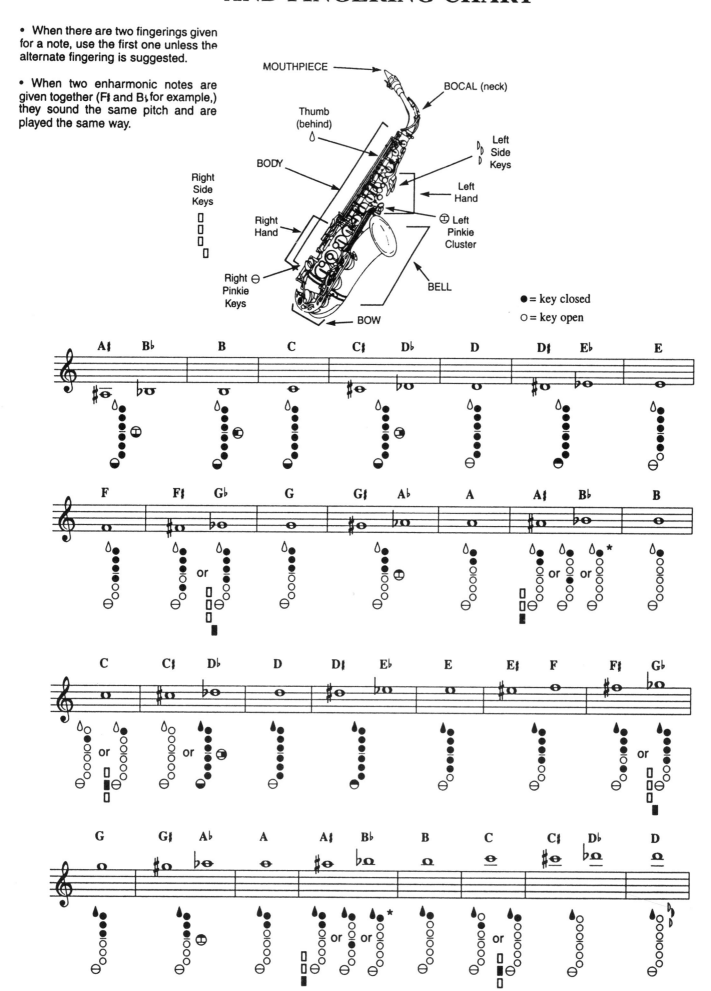

* Both pearl keys are pressed with the Left Hand 1st finger.